THIS IS NOT A BOOK

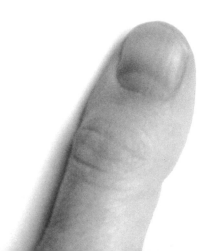

KERI SMITH

A PERIGEE ~~BOOK~~

A PERIGEE BOOK
PUBLISHED BY THE PENGUIN GROUP
PENGUIN GROUP (USA) INC.
375 HUDSON STREET, NEW YORK, NEW YORK 10014, USA
PENGUIN GROUP (CANADA), 90 EGLINTON AVENUE EAST, SUITE 700, TORONTO, ONTARIO M4P 2Y3,
CANADA (A DIVISION OF PEARSON PENGUIN CANADA INC.) • PENGUIN BOOKS LTD., 80 STRAND,
LONDON WC2R ORL, ENGLAND • PENGUIN GROUP IRELAND, 25 ST. STEPHEN'S GREEN, DUBLIN 2, IRELAND
(A DIVISION OF PENGUIN BOOKS LTD.) • PENGUIN GROUP (AUSTRALIA), 250 CAMBERWELL ROAD,
CAMBERWELL, VICTORIA 3124, AUSTRALIA (A DIVISION OF PEARSON AUSTRALIA GROUP PTY. LTD.) •
PENGUIN BOOKS INDIA PVT. LTD., 11 COMMUNITY CENTRE, PANCHSHEEL PARK, NEW DELHI--110 017,
INDIA • PENGUIN GROUP (NZ), 67 APOLLO DRIVE, ROSEDALE, AUCKLAND 0632, NEW ZEALAND
(A DIVISION OF PEARSON NEW ZEALAND LTD.) • PENGUIN BOOKS (SOUTH AFRICA) (PTY.) LTD.,
24 STURDEE AVENUE, ROSEBANK, JOHANNESBURG 2196, SOUTH AFRICA

PENGUIN BOOKS LTD., REGISTERED OFFICES: 80 STRAND, LONDON WC2R ORL, ENGLAND

THE PUBLISHER DOES NOT HAVE ANY CONTROL OVER AND DOES NOT ASSUME ANY RESPONSIBILITY
FOR AUTHOR OR THIRD-PARTY WEBSITES OR THEIR CONTENT.

THIS IS NOT A BOOK

FIRST EDITION: SEPTEMBER 2009

ISBN: 978-0-399-53521-5

PRINTED IN THE UNITED STATES OF AMERICA

20   19   18   17   16   15   14   13   12   11

NOTE TO THE READER/USER

You are about to embark on a journey. You have come to this page because the object you now hold in your hands has piqued your curiosity. You may not know exactly what it is, but that is precisely the point. In order to complete it you will be asked to do a number of things. Many of these things require the use of your imagination. You are welcome to alter this journey in any way you choose. You may complete the tasks in any time frame. Try things at different speeds to see how they change, using whatever materials you have on hand. If anything happens during the course of <u>This Is Not a Book</u> that you do not like, you may go back and alter it or remove it completely. You may add things you think it might need. It is your work. There are some things you need to remember:

1. TRUST IN YOUR IMAGINATION. IT IS THE SOURCE OF ALL TRUE JOURNEYS.

2. THINGS ARE NOT ALWAYS WHAT THEY SEEM.

3. ANYTHING CAN HAPPEN.

THIS IS AN INCONVENIENCE.

TAKE THIS IS NOT A BOOK
EVERYWHERE YOU GO FOR
ONE WEEK. YOU MUST
PLACE IT IN FULL VIEW
AT ALL TIMES.

1

THIS IS A RECORDING

RECORD THE EVENTS
OF YOUR DAY IN POINT
FORM HERE:

-
-
-
-
-
-
-
-

DEVICE.

MAKE A MARK FOR
EVERY TIME YOU ENTER
A ROOM.

THIS IS A SECRET AGENT.*

INSTRUCTIONS: GIVE <u>THIS IS NOT</u>
<u>A BOOK</u> SOME KIND OF DISGUISE TO
HIDE ITS IDENTITY.
*DISPOSE OF THIS NOTE AFTER READING.

THIS IS A TEST OF ENDURANCE.

1. HOLD <u>THIS IS NOT A BOOK</u> ABOVE YOUR HEAD FOR AS LONG AS POSSIBLE.

2. WRITE YOUR TIME HERE: _____.

THIS IS A

8

NATURE EMULATOR.

TAKE A BREAK ANYWHERE YOU ARE.

*ADD SOME IMAGERY TO THIS SCENE.

9

THIS

IS

A

CHALLENGE.

PART 1:

MAKE

THIS

PAGE

AS

BIG

AS

POSSIBLE.

THIS IS A CHALLENGE.
PART 2:
MAKE THIS PAGE AS
SMALL AS POSSIBLE.

11

THIS IS A **THOUGHT GARDEN.**

RUMOR HAS IT, IF YOU PLANT SEEDS (IDEAS) IN THE DIRT THEY WILL GROW AND BECOME TRUE TO LIFE IN THE REAL WORLD.

PLANT YOUR IDEAS HERE.

THIS IS AN ANNOYANCE.

DO SEVERAL THINGS TO THIS PAGE
TO MAKE IT ANNOYING (E.G., MAKE
IT STICKY, WRITE AN INSULT, ETC.).

15

THIS IS A **PORTABLE**

DOODLE HERE WHILE
YOU BRAINSTORM YOUR
NEXT BIG IDEA.

PEN GOES HERE.

*OPEN THIS PAGE
SO IT SITS FLAT.

WORKSTATION.

ATTACH IMPORTANT
DOCUMENTS:

COFFEE OR
TEA GOES
HERE.

NOTES

- - - - - - - - - -
- - - - - - - - - -
- - - - - - - - - -
- - - - - - - - - -
- - - - - - - - - -
- - - - - - - - - -
- - - - - - - - - -
- - - - - - - - - -

THIS IS A CHOICE.

1. PICK A NUMBER BETWEEN 1 AND 221.
2. GO TO THAT PAGE.
3. FLIP FORWARD FIVE PAGES. (IF YOU CANNOT, THEN FLIP BACK FIVE PAGES.)
4. DO WHATEVER IS ON THAT PAGE <u>IMMEDIATELY</u>.

20

THIS IS A TRANSFORMATION.

COME UP WITH A WAY TO PERMANENTLY ALTER THIS PAGE. AND CHANGE IT INTO SOMETHING COMPLETELY DIFFERENT.

THIS IS A DISAPPEARANCE.

1. DRAW OR WRITE SOMETHING HERE.
2. ERASE IT SOMEHOW (E.G., PENCIL & ERASER, WATER-SOLUBLE INK, SANDPAPER).

THIS IS A LIMITED EDITION ART PIECE.

1. EXECUTE AN IDEA ON EACH OF THESE
SQUARES (IT COULD BE A DRAWING OR A THOUGHT).
2. SIGN AND DATE EACH PIECE ON THE BACK.
3. CUT THEM OUT. 4. DISPLAY THEM IN PUBLIC
WITH A SIGN THAT SAYS "LIMITED EDITION ART
PIECES: FREE." 5. CHECK BACK TO SEE IF
ANYONE HAS TAKEN THEM.

* YOU CAN ALSO WEAR A BADGE THAT SAYS ARTIST
AND STAND NEAR THE ARTWORK.

THIS IS A

BLANK SPACE.

THINK OF NOTHING.
HOW MANY EXAMPLES OF NOTHING
CAN YOU THINK OF?
DRAW NOTHING HERE.

THIS IS A VOYAGE.

1. CUT OUT PAGE.
2. FOLLOW FOLDING INSTRUCTIONS BELOW.
3. PUT IN WATER.

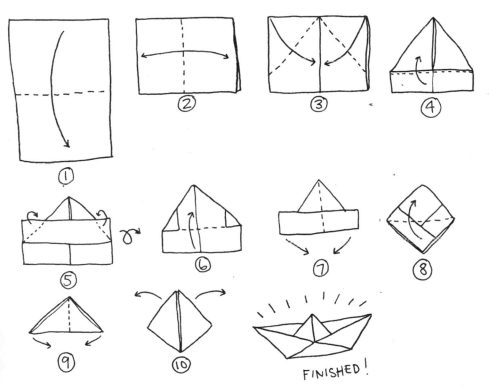

FINISHED!

THIS IS A SECRET IDENTITY.

SECRET IDENTITY PROFILE
(WHO WOULD YOU LIKE TO BE?)

NAME:
PLACE OF BIRTH:
DATE OF BIRTH:
PROFESSION:
LIKES:

DISLIKES:

LOCATION:

LIFESTYLE SYNOPSIS (DAILY ACTIVITIES):

PERSONAL HABITS:

HOBBIES:

GROUPS & ASSOCIATIONS:

SOCIAL LIFE:

CUT OUT

CUT OUT

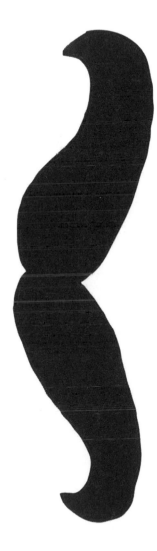

31

THIS IS A SCAVENGER HUNT.

HERE IS A LIST OF THINGS FOR YOU TO FIND:

A SEED POD

THE DEFINITION OF A WORD YOU DON'T KNOW

A PUZZLE TO COMPLETE

A SECRET CODE

A SCIENTIFIC THEOREM

SOMETHING RED

SOMETHING THAT WAS ALIVE

A MAP

A FOOTNOTE

SOMETHING THAT WAS LOST

A PIECE OF THREAD

A TICKET STUB

SOMETHING WITH A CIRCLE ON IT

A PALINDROME

A PIECE OF TOILET PAPER (UNUSED)

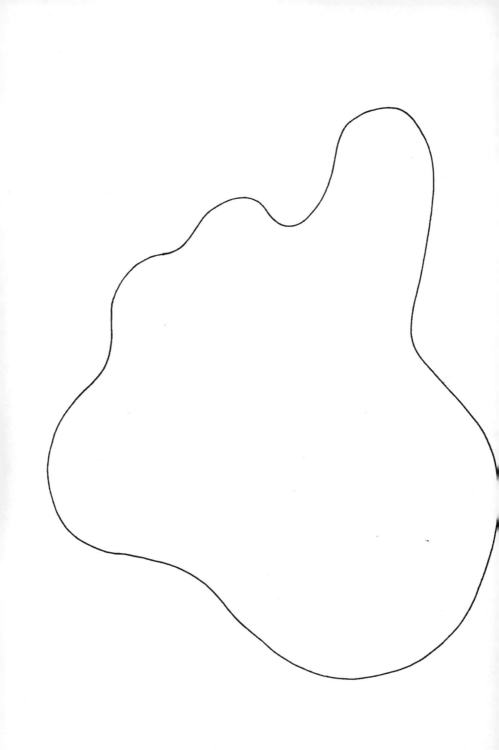

34

THIS IS A PLAYGROUND.

COLOR IN THIS SHAPE USING THE STRANGEST METHOD YOU CAN THINK OF (E.G., MAKE YOUR WRITING UTENSIL REALLY LONG BY ATTACHING SOMETHING TO IT WITH TAPE).

THIS IS A CHAIN LETTER.

1. CUT OUT THE LETTER.
2. UNDER "ORIGINATOR" PUT YOUR NAME & ADDRESS.
3. SEND LETTER TO ONE FRIEND.

DEAR FRIEND,

THIS IS A CHAIN LETTER.
IT'S ONLY PURPOSE IS TO SEE
HOW FAR IT CAN GO.
ADD YOUR NAME AND LOCATION
TO THE BOTTOM OF THE LIST.
THEN SEND THE LETTER TO
ONE FRIEND.

ORIGINATOR: _ _ _ _ _ _ _ _ _ _ _
_ _ _ _ _ _ _ _ _
_ _ _ _ _ _ _ _ _
_ _ _ _ _ _ _ _ _ _ _ _ _ _ _ _ _ _ _
_ _ _ _ _ _ _ _ _ _ _ _ _ _ _ _ _ _ _
_ _ _ _ _ _ _ _ _ _ _ _ _ _ _ _ _ _ _

THIS IS A COMMENT.

1. FILL IN A THOUGHT.
2. LEAVE IN A PUBLIC PLACE.

40

THIS IS AN ACTION SCULPTURE.
COME UP WITH AN INTERESTING WAY
TO MAKE THIS IS NOT A BOOK MOVE
(E.G., TIE AN UMBRELLA TO THE SPINE.
DROP FROM A HEIGHT).

THIS IS A SET OF DIRECTIONS.

1. GET A WRITING UTENSIL (PEN, PENCIL, ETC.).
2. CHOOSE A STARTING POINT.
3. DRAW A STRAIGHT LINE IN ANY DIRECTION; STOP BEFORE YOU GET TO THE EDGE OF THE PAGE.
4. DRAW A CURVY LINE IN THE OPPOSITE DIRECTION.
5. ADD A SQUARE. COLOR IT IN.
6. FROM ONE OF THE CORNERS OF THE SQUARE DRAW A DOTTED LINE ON A DIAGONAL, ABOUT TWO INCHES LONG.
7. AT THE END OF THE DOTTED LINE DRAW A CIRCLE.
8. INSIDE THE CIRCLE WRITE THE NAME OF THE LAST PERSON YOU SPOKE TO.
9. FROM THE CIRCLE DRAW A LINE TO ONE OF THE CORNERS OF THE PAGE.
10. FOLD THE CORNER DOWN AND COLOR IT IN.
11. FROM THAT CORNER DRAW A VERY FAT LINE TO THE MIDDLE OF THE PAGE.
12. DRAW THE MOON HERE.
13. SIGN YOUR NAME.

THIS IS A FRIEND.

TURN <u>THIS IS NOT A BOOK</u> OR OTHER OBJECTS INTO CHARACTERS BY ADDING THESE ITEMS.

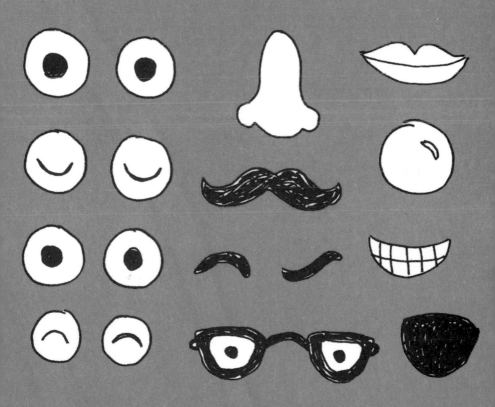

*PHOTO IS ACTUAL SIZE.

THIS IS A FACTORY

THAT CREATES VERY SMALL BOOKS BY UNKNOWN AUTHORS.

THE FACTORY ITSELF IS VERY SMALL.*

1. CUT OUT TEMPLATE BELOW ALONG SOLID LINES.
2. ASSEMBLE ACCORDING TO DIAGRAM.
3. ADD CONTENT.
4. CONTINUE PRODUCTION.

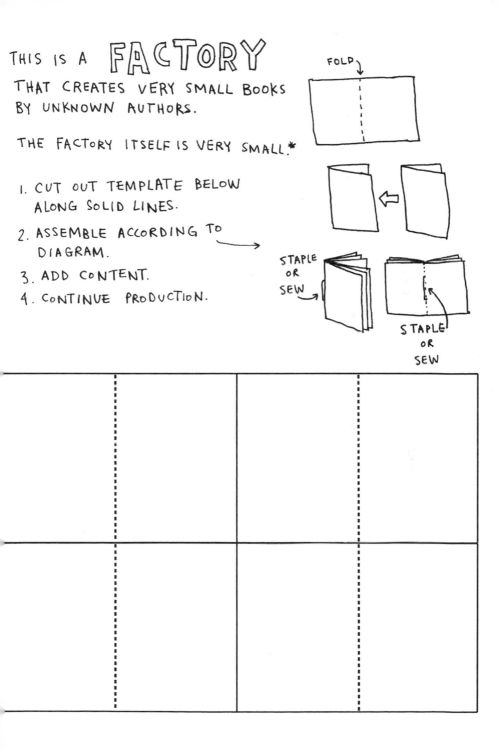

FOLD

STAPLE OR SEW

STAPLE OR SEW

THIS IS A FORM OF communication.

1. WRITE A MESSAGE FOR SOMEONE HERE.
2. GIVE MESSAGE TO RECIPIENT.
3. WAIT FOR RESPONSE.
4. PASS <u>THIS IS NOT A BOOK</u> BACK AND
   FORTH.*

*IF THE RECIPIENT LIVES FAR AWAY, MAIL

<u>THIS IS NOT A BOOK</u> BACK AND FORTH.   50

THIS IS A CONCEALMENT.
USE THIS PAGE TO COVER UP A
PAGE THAT YOU DON'T LIKE.

THIS IS A HIDING PLACE.

STASH YOUR SECRETS HERE.

THIS IS AN IMAGINARY *place*.

THIS IS YOUR VERY OWN PLANET.
YOU MUST ADD THINGS TO IT TO MAKE
IT FLOURISH.
1. CREATE A LEGEND WITH SYMBOLS
TO ADD BUILDINGS, PEOPLE, AND THINGS
FROM YOUR IMAGINATION.
2. DESRIBE THE WEATHER AND THE INHABITANTS;
ADD ROADS, ETC.

56

THIS IS A TIME TRAVEL DEVICE

1. THINK OF A TIME AND PLACE YOU
   WOULD LIKE TO REVISIT. ENTER IT
   ON THE SCREEN BELOW.

ENTER TIME AND PLACE:

2. MAKE DETAILED NOTES INCLUDING
   EVERYTHING YOU CAN REMEMBER
   ABOUT THAT TIME—COLORS, SMELLS,
   LIGHT, TIME OF DAY, NAMES, SPACE.

ALTERNATE: WRITE ABOUT A FUTURE
TIME AND PLACE USING YOUR
IMAGINATION.

THIS IS AN

ETHNOGRAPHIC STUDY.

1. GO TO A PUBLIC PLACE.
2. PRETEND YOU ARE AN ALIEN VISITING THE PLANET FOR THE FIRST TIME.
3. TAKE NOTES ABOUT HUMAN BEHAVIOR AND HUMAN CUSTOMS AS IF YOU'VE NEVER SEEN THEM BEFORE.

60

THIS IS A COMMITMENT.

DO ONE THING ON THIS LIST EVERY DAY
FOR ONE MONTH.

WEAR AN ARTICLE OF CLOTHING INSIDE OUT
READ A BOOK YOU DON'T THINK YOU WILL LIKE
SING ON YOUR WAY TO WORK/SCHOOL
GIVE SOMETHING AWAY
TAKE A PHOTO
DRAW SOMETHING
WRITE A LETTER

63

THIS IS A RANDOM OCCURRENCE.

1. DROP A STRING ONTO THIS PAGE.
2. TRACE THE STRING.
3. REPEAT.

THIS IS A CONTAINER.

DEFINITION: CON•TAIN•ER NOUN AN OBJECT
THAT CAN BE USED TO HOLD OR
TRANSPORT SOMETHING.

USE THIS IS NOT A BOOK TO TRANSPORT
AN UNLIKELY OBJECT OF YOUR CHOOSING.

THIS IS A LOST TREASURE.

1. FIND A GOOD HIDING SPOT FOR THIS IS NOT A BOOK.
2. CREATE A "TREASURE MAP."
3. GIVE THE MAP TO A FRIEND AND INSTRUCT THEM
   TO FIND IT.

APPLICATION FOR PAGE USAGE

TO BE COMPLETED BY APPLICANT (PLEASE PRINT*):

SECTION 1

APPLICANT'S NAME _____ PHONE(S) (PLEASE LIST ALL PHONE

NUMBERS YOU HAVE EVER HAD)**_____ SHOE SIZE _____

ADDRESS _____ BIRTHDAY _____

MOTHER'S MAIDEN NAME _____ MOTHER'S MOTHER'S MOTHER'S

MAIDEN NAME _____ FAVORITE COLOR _____

TIME YOU WENT TO SLEEP LAST FRIDAY NIGHT _____ DOMINANT HAND L R

CIRCLE DAY OF THE WEEK M T W TH F S S

SECTION 2

PLEASE STATE THE REASON YOU ARE APPLYING FOR USAGE OF THIS PAGE.

_____

PLEASE DESCRIBE WHAT YOU HAD FOR BREAKFAST THIS MORNING.

_____

PLEASE WRITE YOUR BEST FRIEND'S NAME WHILE TOUCHING YOUR NOSE.

_____

STATE THE LAST TIME YOU FILLED OUT A FORM. FOR WHAT PURPOSE?

_____

SECTION 3

DRAW AN OFFICIAL STAMP HERE.

INSTRUCTIONS**

1. STAPLE A PHOTO OF YOURSELF TO THIS FORM.

2. CUT OUT SECTION 3 AND ATTACH IT TO PAGE 32 OF THIS IS NOT A BOOK.

3. SIGN AND DATE THIS FORM.

4. PLEASE FILL OUT THIS FORM IN TRIPLICATE.

5. IN ORDER TO PROCESS THIS FORM YOU MUST HAVE THE BLESSING OF A NEIGHBOR

*INCORRECT SPELLING WILL VOID APPLICATION.

**IF ANSWERS DO NOT FIT IN SPACE ALLOTTED, PLEASE ATTACH AN ADDITIONAL

FORM.

OFFICE COPY   FORM #253HD459208

THIS IS A BUREAUCRACY.

1. FILL OUT THIS FORM.

2. FOLLOW INSTRUCTIONS AT BOTTOM OF FORM.

THIS IS A BORDER.

PLACE THIS IN A LOCATION IN WHICH
YOU WOULD LIKE TO MAKE A SEPARATION
BETWEEN TWO AREAS. YOU MAY WISH
TO WRITE A NOTE ON EACH SIDE EXPLAINING
WHAT THE SPACE IS DESIGNATED FOR
(E.G., PUBLIC VS. PRIVATE, MINE VS. YOURS).

THIS IS AN EMBELLISHMENT.
USE THIS FRAME TO EMBELLISH ANOTHER
PAGE.

74

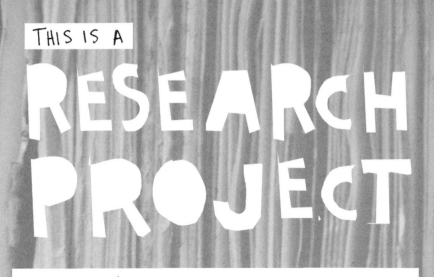

THIS IS A
RESEARCH PROJECT

1. FIND AN ENCYCLOPEDIA.
2. OPEN IT UP TO A RANDOM PAGE.
3. CLOSE YOUR EYES AND POINT.
4. WRITE DOWN THE SUBJECT YOU HAVE CHOSEN.
5. FIND OUT MORE ABOUT THIS SUBJECT. WRITE DOWN ANY FACTS YOU FIND. BECOME AN EXPERT.

76

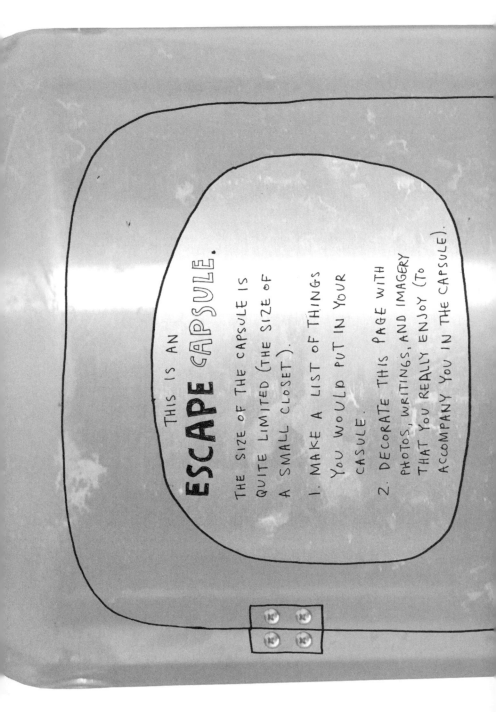

THIS IS AN

ESCAPE CAPSULE.

THE SIZE OF THE CAPSULE IS QUITE LIMITED (THE SIZE OF A SMALL CLOSET).

1. MAKE A LIST OF THINGS YOU WOULD PUT IN YOUR CASULE.

2. DECORATE THIS PAGE WITH PHOTOS, WRITINGS, AND IMAGERY THAT YOU REALLY ENJOY (TO ACCOMPANY YOU IN THE CAPSULE).

77

THIS IS A GROUP ACTIVITY.

1. ASSEMBLE A GROUP OF PEOPLE.
2. WHILE STANDING, HAVE A CONTEST
TO SEE WHO CAN BALANCE <u>THIS</u>
<u>IS NOT A BOOK</u> ON SOME PART OF
THEIR BODY (EXCLUDING THE HEAD)
FOR THE LONGEST PERIOD OF
TIME.

ALTERNATE: WHILE WALKING, PLACE
THIS IS NOT A BOOK BETWEEN YOUR
LEGS. SEE WHO CAN WALK THE
FARTHEST.

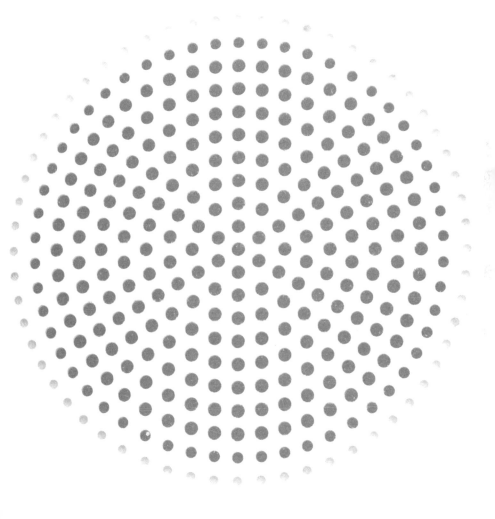

THIS IS A *guest registry.**

* FOR FRIENDS OR VISITORS

YOUR COMMENTS ARE MOST WELCOME.

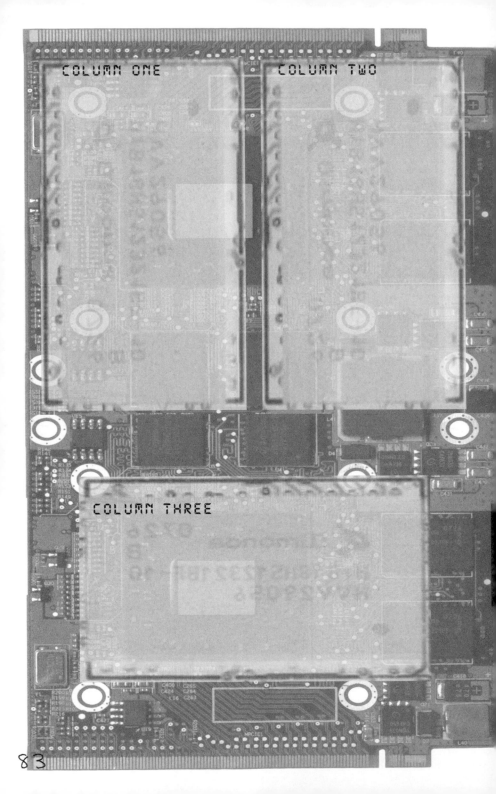

COLUMN ONE

COLUMN TWO

COLUMN THREE

THIS IS AN

IDEA FORMULATION GENERATOR.

1. IN COLUMN ONE MAKE A LIST OF THINGS FOUND IN NATURE.

2. IN COLUMN TWO MAKE A LIST OF OBJECTS YOU USE EVERY DAY.

3. IN COLUMN THREE MAKE A LIST OF WORDS YOU LIKE.

4. PICK ONE ITEM FROM EACH LIST AND COMBINE THEM TO COME UP WITH AN IDEA FOR A NEW PRODUCT OR CONCEPT.

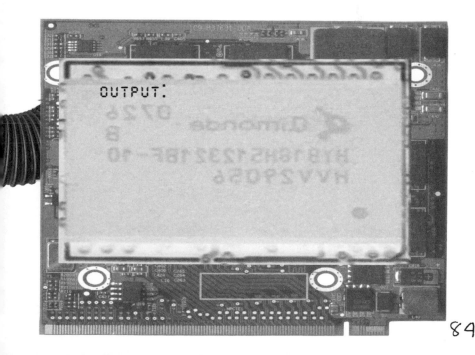

OUTPUT:

THIS IS A GROUPING OF CIRCLES
WITH NO PURPOSE WHATSOEVER.

DRAW THEM USING WHATEVER METHODS
YOU PREFER.

86

THIS A # METHODOLOGY

FOR INVESTIGATING THE PRACTICE OF
CARRYING THINGS THAT ARE NOT BOOKS.

1. TEST EACH OF THESE METHODS.
2. COME UP WITH FIVE MORE.

THIS IS A HABITAT.

FOR MICROORGANISMS. PLEASE HELP THEM TO FEEL AT HOME BY ADDING A VARIETY OF THINGS (FURNITURE, ROOMS, HOUSES, WALKWAYS, ETC.). MAKE THEM AS SMALL AS POSSIBLE.

THIS IS A TELEVISION.
YOU GET TO DO ALL YOUR OWN
PROGRAMMING.

1. WRITE YOUR OWN SHOW.
2. MAKE A THREE-DIMENSIONAL
   DIORAMA OF YOUR SHOW OUT
   OF CARDBOARD.
3. USE THE TV AS A FRAME.

THIS IS
A DARE.

WRITE A LIST OF THINGS
YOU WOULD LIKE TO TRY
IN YOUR LIFETIME.

94

95

THIS IS A

WISHING WELL.

1. WRITE A WISH.
2. TAPE MONEY HERE.

AAAAAVVVVVMMMMMTTTTT
WWWWMMMMRRRRRRGGGGGGG
IIIIIIOOOOOOOLLLLLLLWWWWW
QQQQQQNNNNNNCCCCCCSSSSSS
DDDDDDEEEEEEEEFFFFFFFJJJJJJJ
SSSS THISISAHIDDENMESSAGE OO
HHHHHEEEEEEEWWWWWPPPP
AAAAAABBBBBBBBKKKKKKKFFFFF
NNNN FINDAWAYTOHIDEAMESSA
GESOMEWHEREINTHISISNOTABO
OKSOTHATNOONECANFINDIT AAA
TTTTTUUUUUUUPPPPPPPHHHH
SSSSSS GOODLUCK AAAAANNNN
KKKKKKKKKEEEEEEEEAAAAAAA
NNNNNNSSSSSSSWWWWWEEEE
YYYYYYYIIIIIIIOOOOOOOXXXXX
RRRRRREEEEEEEEAAAAADDDD
MMMMOOOOOOOOORRRRREEEE
BBBBBBBOOOOOOOOOOOKKKKK
SSSSSSSSEEEEEEEAAAATTTTT
YYYYYYOOOOOOOOUUUUURRR
GGGGGGGGRRRRRREEEEEEEE
NNNNNSSSSSSYYYYYOOOOUUU
AAAARRRRRREEEEEEGGGGGG
RRRREEEEEEAAAAATTTTTT

98

THIS IS AN EXPERIMENT.
LEAVE THIS IS NOT A BOOK
SOMEWHERE OVERNIGHT.

THIS IS A MAP.

CREATE A MAP BASED ON SOME ASPECT
OF YOUR EVERYDAY LIFE. SOME
EXAMPLES MIGHT BE YOUR DESK,
YOUR WALK TO SCHOOL OR WORK,
YOUR DINNER TABLE, YOUR HAND.

THIS IS A PSYCHOLOGICAL MOOD-ALTERING MACHINE.

1. WRITE ABOUT YOUR CURRENT MOOD IN DETAIL IN THE SPACE PROVIDED.

2. ENTER YOUR MOOD OF CHOICE ON THE MACHINE BELOW

3. FOCUS REALLY HARD ON WHAT YOUR MOOD OF CHOICE FEELS LIKE.

4. ALLOW FOR MOOD TRANSITION TO TAKE PLACE. (MAY TAKE A FEW HOURS.)

CURRENT MOOD:

THIS IS A VIRTUAL REALITY.

1. MAKE A LIST OF YOUR PERSONALITY TRAITS.
2. TAKE THOSE TRAITS AND EXAGGERATE OR
   EMBELLISH THEM. CREATE A CHARACTER (OR AVATAR)
   WITH THESE TRAITS AS SUPERPOWERS.
3. CREATE SEVERAL SUPERHERO ACCESORIES.

EXAMPES: HER EXCELLENT ORGANIZATIONAL SKILLS
         MAKE HER FULLY PREPARED FOR EVERY
         POTENTIAL CRISIS, HE REPELS ENEMIES
         WITH HIS LOVE OF GARLIC, SHE HAS
         A GREAT ABILITY TO FIND THINGS
         IN MESSY SPACES, HE IS A
         TIMING EXPERT.

106

THIS IS A TOP SECRET DOCUMENT.

1. FIND A DICTIONARY.
2. WRITE A MESSAGE USING THIS CODE.
3. CUT THE CODE OUT AND HIDE IT SOMEWHERE
   IN <u>THIS IS NOT A BOOK.</u>
4. GIVE IT TO A FRIEND TO SOLVE.

<u>N + 7</u>
REPLACE EVERY
NOUN IN A TEXT
WITH THE NOUN
SEVEN ENTRIES
AFTER IT IN A
DICTIONARY.
THE MORE NOUNS
YOU USE, THE
MORE CRYPTIC IT
WILL BE.

THIS IS AN EXCERPT FROM *another book.*

1. PULL A BOOK OFF YOUR BOOKSHELF (OR ONE AT A LIBRARY).
2. OPEN IT TO A RANDOM PAGE.
3. WRITE THE FIRST SENTENCE YOU SEE HERE.

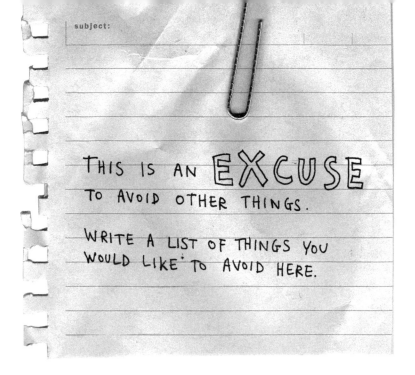

subject:

THIS IS AN EXCUSE
TO AVOID OTHER THINGS.

WRITE A LIST OF THINGS YOU
WOULD LIKE TO AVOID HERE.

THIS IS AN INTERVIEW.

WHAT IS YOUR FULL NAME?

WHAT IS YOUR FAVORITE THING TO EAT?

DESCRIBE THE TASTE OF YOUR FAVORITE FOOD
WITHOUT COMPARING IT TO OTHER FOODS.

WHAT ARE YOUR FAVORITE THINGS TO DO?

113

WHO ARE YOUR FAVORITE PEOPLE?

WHAT WAS YOUR FAVORITE THING TO DO WHEN YOU WERE REALLY LITTLE?

DESCRIBE YOUR FAVORITE OUTFIT.

WHERE DO YOU SEE YOURSELF IN FIVE YEARS?

THIS IS A NETWORK.

CREATE AN ARRANGEMENT OF INTERSECTING
LINES GOING EVERY WHICH WAY.

116

THIS IS A
PUBLIC SPACE.

INVITE PEOPLE TO ADD SOMETHING
TO THIS PAGE.

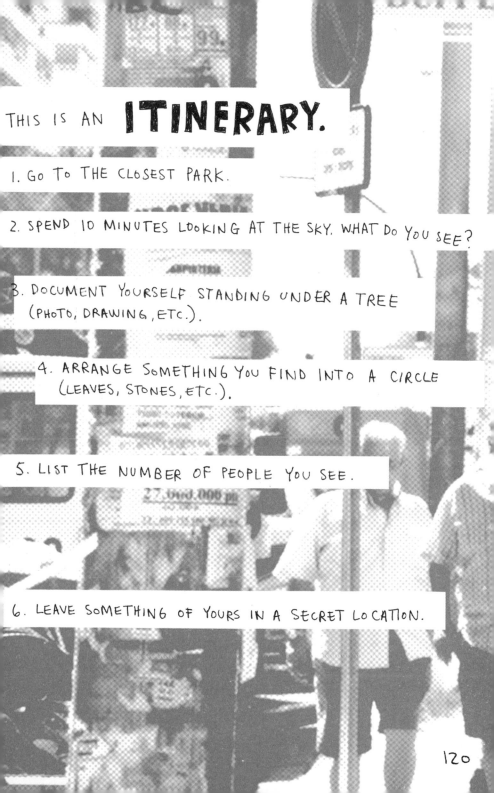

THIS IS AN **ITINERARY.**

1. GO TO THE CLOSEST PARK.

2. SPEND 10 MINUTES LOOKING AT THE SKY. WHAT DO YOU SEE?

3. DOCUMENT YOURSELF STANDING UNDER A TREE (PHOTO, DRAWING, ETC.).

4. ARRANGE SOMETHING YOU FIND INTO A CIRCLE (LEAVES, STONES, ETC.).

5. LIST THE NUMBER OF PEOPLE YOU SEE.

6. LEAVE SOMETHING OF YOURS IN A SECRET LOCATION.

THIS IS A **WINDOW.**

1. CUT OUT HOLE.
2. PLACE IN FRONT OF DESIRED VIEW.
3. SIT.

CUT OUT

122

THIS IS A MOMENT IN TIME.
THIS DAY WILL NEVER HAPPEN AGAIN.
DOCUMENT ITS PASSING.

THIS IS AN UNDERGROUND ORGANIZATION.

1. GO TO WWW.THISISNOTABOOK.ORG.
2. ENTER THIS CODE: JTZ5261.
3. RECEIVE YOUR MISSION.

SUBMIT

127

THIS IS A MATERIAL.

CONDUCT SOME EXPERIMENTS TO UNCOVER THE PROPERTIES OF THIS PAGE (PAPER). MAKE A LIST AND TEST ALL OF THE THINGS YOU CAN DO TO IT. WHAT HAPPENS WHEN YOU ADD THINGS (SUBSTANCES) TO IT?

THIS IS A
PORTABLE
HOLE/PORTAL.

MAKES THINGS DISAPPEAR AT WILL.

1. CUT OUT.
2. AFFIX THE HOLE TO ANY SURFACE.
3. USE.

IF YOU COULD BE ANYWHERE YOU WANT
RIGHT NOW, WHERE WOULD IT BE?

130

THIS IS A PERFORMANCE.

CHOOSE ONE

SELECT A PIECE OF WRITING YOU REALLY LIKE. READ IT OUT LOUD, WHERE OTHERS CAN HEAR YOU.

WHILE IN A PUBLIC PLACE, DRAW A LARGE CIRCLE IN FULL VIEW. COLOR IT IN.

THIS IS A # MULTIDIRECTIONAL UNIT.

1. GO TO A PLACE YOU WOULD LIKE TO EXPLORE.
2. OPEN THIS IS NOT A BOOK FLAT.
3. PLACE ON GROUND (OR FLOOR). SPIN.*
4. MOVE IN THE DIRECTION OF THE ARROW.
5. REPEAT WHENEVER A CHOICE OF
   DIRECTION PRESENTS ITSELF (E.G. INTERSECTION).

* IF SURFACE DOES NOT ALLOW SPINNING, PLACE
  THIS IS NOT A BOOK ON A LARGE PIECE OF CARDBOARD.

THIS IS AN INVENTORY
OF YOUR THINGS.

1. MAKE A LIST OF ITEMS YOU OWN.

2. BESIDE EACH ITEM PUT THE QUANTITY OF ITEMS (I.E., BOOKS: 432, PANTS: 4).

THIS IS A CELEBRATION.

CREATE A HOMEMADE CELEBRATION USING WHATEVER YOU HAVE AROUND YOU.

1. COME UP WITH SOME KIND OF THEME.

2. MAKE A FESTIVE MEAL, DISH, OR DESSERT.

3. PLAY MUSIC YOU LIKE.

4. A SPECIAL OUTFIT OR COSTUME ALWAYS HELPS. INVITE FRIENDS.

5. USING MAGAZINES, NEWSPAPERS, OR COLORED PAPER, CUT OUT A NUMBER OF TRIANGLES AND ATTACH TO STRING FOR A BANNER.

THIS IS A PLATE.

PLACE YOUR DINNER HERE.

146

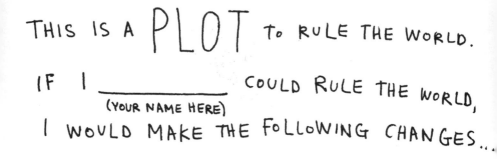

THIS IS A PLOT TO RULE THE WORLD.

IF I _____ COULD RULE THE WORLD,
(YOUR NAME HERE)

I WOULD MAKE THE FOLLOWING CHANGES...

THIS IS A

COME UP WITH 50 DIFFERENT
WAYS <u>THIS IS NOT A BOOK</u>
COULD BE USED AS A TOOL
OR UTENSIL OF SOME KIND.

TOOL.

TOOL |toōl|
NOUN
A DEVICE OR IMPLEMENT, ESP.
ONE HELD IN THE HAND, USED
TO CARRY OUT A PARTICULAR
FUNCTION.

THIS IS A CUSTOMIZABLE OBJECT.

ADD YOUR OWN FEATURES TO <u>THIS IS NOT A BOOK.</u> SOME IDEAS: COLOR IN SOME PAGES, SHAPE THE PAGES WITH SCISSORS, ADD STRIPES, GLUE IN ENVELOPES FOR COLLECTING THINGS, ADD AN ELASTIC BAND TO HOLD IT CLOSED, MAKE YOUR OWN BOOKMARK, WRITE NOTES IN BLANK SPACES, FOLD DOWN CORNERS, COLOR THE EDGES OF THE PAGES, ADD A GRID, ADD A MAP OF YOUR CITY, ADD LINES, ADD STICKERS, MAKE SOME KIND OF CARRYING CASE FOR IT.

THIS OBJECT BELONGS TO:

HERE ARE SOME
NOTE TABS FOR
YOU TO CUT OUT
AND GLUE ON.

CUSTOMIZED BY: _____

BOOKMARK

146

THIS IS A SYSTEM. CHOOSE ONE WORD FROM EACH PAGE OF THIS IS NOT A BOOK TO FORM A VERY LONG SENTENCE.

THIS IS MAIL.

CUT OUT, GLUE ONTO CARDBOARD,
AND MAIL TO A FRIEND.

THIS IS NOT A BOOK.
THIS IS A POSTCARD.

THIS IS A

DO SOMETHING TO THIS PAGE
TO MAKE IT SO PEOPLE WILL
WANT TO AVOID IT.

THIS IS A FORM OF MOVEMENT.

DOCUMENT SOME KIND OF MOVEMENT HERE (E.G., TAPPING WITH A PEN, RUNNING AND JUMPING WITH A PENCIL, WALKING, ETC.).

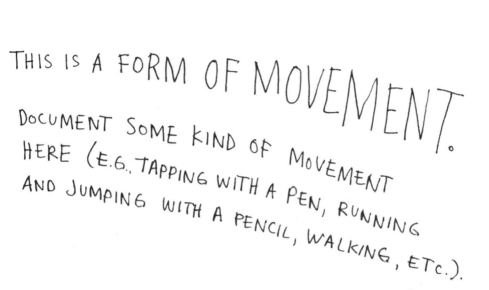

A UPC BARCODE THAT WAS MOVED WHILE BEING SCANNED.

154

THIS IS A RANDOM ADVENTURE.

1. GO OUTSIDE.

2. WALK UNTIL YOU SEE SOMETHING RED.

3. TAKE TEN STEPS.

4. LOOK DOWN AT YOUR FEET AND DESCRIBE WHAT YOU SEE IN DETAIL.

THIS IS A DREAM CATCHER.
PUT <u>THIS IS NOT A BOOK</u>
NEXT TO YOU WHILE YOU
ARE SLEEPING AND YOUR
DREAMS WILL STICK TO
THE PAGES. (YOU MAY
HAVE TO WRITE THEM
DOWN RIGHT HERE WHEN
YOU WAKE UP.) ⟶

THIS IS A SCHOOL.

IF YOU COULD TEACH ANY CLASS,
WHAT WOULD IT BE?

DESCRIBE THE CURRICULUM, FIELD TRIPS,
GUEST SPEAKERS, ETC.

160

THIS IS AN INSTRUMENT.

1. USING <u>THIS IS NOT A BOOK</u> AS A SOURCE, COME UP WITH AS MANY DIFFERENT SOUNDS AS YOU CAN (E.G. FLIP THE PAGES, BANG IT, ETC.).

2. DOCUMENT YOUR METHODS HERE.

bang
thump
bump
slam!

THIS IS A **SENSORY** STIMULATION UNIT.
1. COLLECT FIVE THINGS, ONE FOR EACH SENSE.
2. AFFIX THEM HERE.

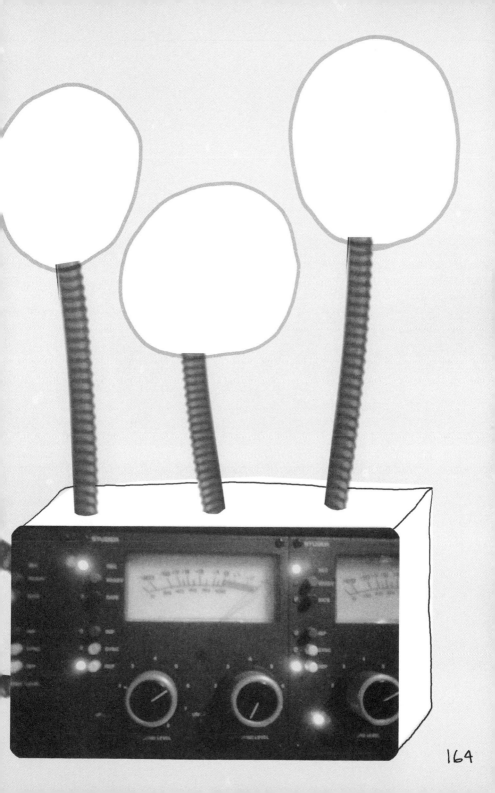

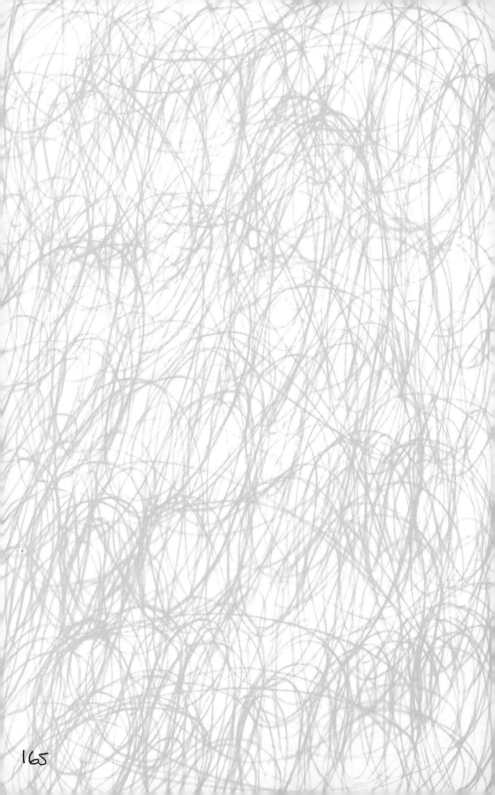

165

THIS IS AN OUTLET.

VENT ABOUT THINGS THAT ARE BOTHERING YOU HERE.
(IF YOU'RE REALLY MAD YOU MIGHT WANT
TO SCRIBBLE UNCONTROLLABLY.)

167

THIS IS A SCULPTURE.

1. USING THIS PAGE CREATE A THREE-DIMENSIONAL OBJECT. YOU MAY COLOR OR ALTER THE PAGE ANY WAY YOU WISH.

2. CREATE A TAG FOR YOUR SCULPTURE.

3. EXHIBIT IT SOMEWHERE.

168

THIS IS A GAME.

1. PLAYERS TAKE TURNS PLACING <u>THIS IS NOT A BOOK</u> IN A DIFFERENT LOCATION FOR EACH ROUND.

2. THERE ARE FIVE ROUNDS. IN EACH ROUND PLAYERS TAKE TURNS RETRIEVING <u>THIS IS NOT A BOOK</u> ACCORDING TO THE REQUIREMENTS ON THE LIST.

   OPTIONAL: TIME EACH ROUND. GIVE EACH PLAYER TWO MINUTES.

   CREATE FIVE MORE REQUIREMENTS (ROUNDS).

ROUND ONE: RETRIEVE <u>THIS IS NOT A BOOK</u> WITH EYES SHUT.

ROUND TWO: RETRIEVE <u>THIS IS NOT A BOOK</u> WITH NO HANDS.

ROUND THREE: CONVINCE A THIRD PARTY TO RETRIEVE <u>THIS IS NOT A BOOK</u> FOR YOU.

ROUND FOUR: RETRIEVE <u>THIS IS NOT A BOOK</u> WHILE STANDING ON ONE LEG.

ROUND FIVE: RETRIEVE <u>THIS IS NOT A BOOK</u> USING A TOOL OR UTENSIL.

THIS IS A CURRENCY.

USE THIS MONEY TO BEGIN YOUR
OWN ECONOMY AND BARTER SYSTEM.

TRADE THIS PAGE FOR ANOTHER ITEM
OF EQUAL OR GREATER VALUE.

DRAW YOUR OWN VERSION OF MONEY.

PLACE A PHOTO
OF YOURSELF HERE

OFFICIAL CURRENCY OF:

(YOUR NAME HERE)

*THIS NOTE IS NOT LEGAL TENDER
BUT IS STILL VAUABLE NONETHELESS.

THIS IS A **PUZZLE.**

CAN YOU MAKE A HOLE IN THIS PAGE
THAT A PERSON CAN PASS THROUGH?

FIND THE ANSWER AT WWW. THIS IS NOT A BOOK.ORG.

174

THIS IS A STRUCTURE.

1. CREATE A STRUCTURE OF SOME KIND COMBINING <u>THIS IS NOT A BOOK</u> WITH OTHER OBJECTS.
2. DOCUMENT IT SOMEHOW.

THIS IS A **KIT** FOR ATTENDING BORING EVENTS.

DRAW A FUNNY FACE.

FIND THESE WORDS AND CIRCLE THEM.

```
-LUFTNEVENUD
MERUXTEDFENE
JNOBTIREDNEA
NDULLETREXXY
OTEAMSSMLOCR
ALANABIVAPID
NRIDSIGRTWTM
LIFELESSOIT
RETSULKCALNS
REAMDVMIGGL
```

UNEVENTFUL
DULL
BLAND
BANAL
LIFELESS
UNEXCITING
DRY
STALE
MUNDANE
TIRED
LACKLUSTER

WRITE A LIST OF
TEN THINGS YOU
CAN SEE RIGHT NOW.

179

THIS IS A *declaration.*

CARVE SOMETHING ONTO THIS TREE.

THIS IS A MIRROR.

CREATE A SELF PORTRAIT
BY DOCUMENTING THE THINGS
THAT DEFINE YOU (CLOTHING,
FOOD, HOBBIES, ETC.). YOU CAN
DRAW, PHOTOGRAPH, OR WRITE
ABOUT THEM HERE.

THIS IS A COLLECTION OF FOUND THINGS.

1. PLACE SOME THINGS THAT YOU FIND ON EACH SHELF.

2. WRITE NOTES ABOUT HOW THEY ARE MAGICAL.

183

THIS IS A CONUNDRUM.

THIS IS AN UNUSUAL PARAGRAPH.
IT IS A CONUNDRUM FOR YOU TO SORT
OUT. HOW QUICKLY CAN YOU FIND OUT
WHAT IS SO UNCOMMON ABOUT IT?
IT LOOKS SO ORDINARY THAT YOU MAY
THINK NOTHING IS ODD ABOUT IT, UNTIL
YOU ACTUALLY MATCH IT AGAINST MOST
PARAGRAPHS THIS LONG. IF YOU PUT
YOUR MIND TO IT AND STUDY IT
HARD, YOU WILL FIND OUT.
NOBODY MAY ASSIST YOU — DO IT
WITHOUT ANY COACHING. GO TO
WORK AND TRY YOUR SKILL AT
FIGURING IT OUT. GOOD LUCK!

FIND THE ANSWER AT WWW.THISISNOTABOOK.ORG.

THIS IS A FORTUNE TELLER.

1. CUT OUT SQUARES.
2. ASK A YES OR NO QUESTION.
3. CLOSE EYES AND PICK A SQUARE FOR YOUR ANSWER.

YES

THIS IS A
MYSTERY

MAYBE

YOU'RE
ON TO
SOMETHING

TRY
AGAIN

NO

189

THIS IS A MYSTERY.
PAGE NUMBER 42 IS MISSING.
WHAT DO YOU THINK HAPPENED
TO IT? WRITE YOUR POSTULATIONS
HERE. SUBMIT THEM TO
WWW.THISISNOTABOOK.ORG.

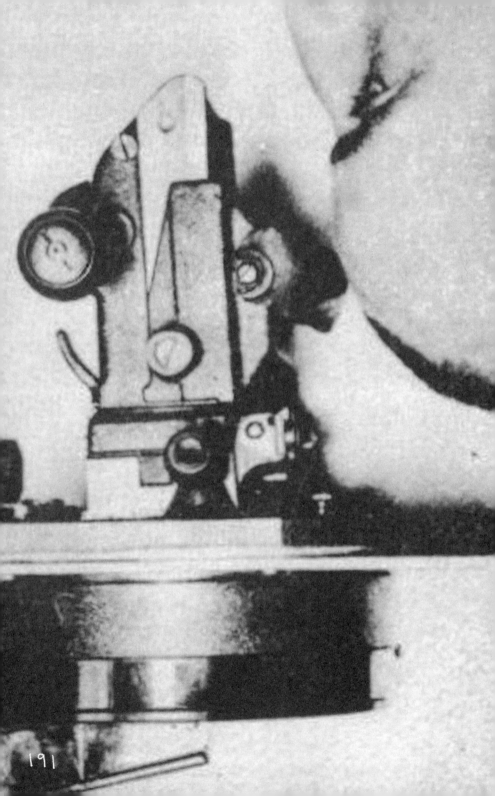

THIS IS A PARALLEL UNIVERSE.

WHAT WOULD YOUR WORLD BE LIKE
IF EVERYTHING WAS THE OPPOSITE
OF WHAT IT IS NOW?

THIS IS AN ACCIDENT.

CHOOSE ONE OF THE FOLLOWING:

1. PLACE A FEW DROPS OF INK ON THE PAGE AND BLOW WITH A STRAW.

2. CUT A BUNCH OF SMALL SHAPES OUT OF COLORED PAPER. DROP THEM ONTO THE PAGE AND GLUE THEM WHERE THEY LAND.

3. PLACE THIS IS NOT A BOOK ON THE FLOOR AND DROP INK ONTO IT WHILE STANDING.

THIS IS A TRAP.

DO SOMETHING OR WRITE SOMETHING
THAT WILL MAKE SOMEONE ELSE WANT
TO PICK UP THIS IS NOT A BOOK.

THIS IS A STREAM OF CONSCIOUSNESS
WHAT ARE YOU THINK
ABOUT RIGHT NOW?

198

THIS IS A **LANDSCAPE.**

FIND A WAY TO MAKE THIS PAGE BLEND COMPLETELY WITH OR FIT INTO A ROOM OR LANDSCAPE OF YOUR CHOOSING.

200

THIS IS A CHANCE OPERATION.

1. CUT OUT GRID.
2. PLACE IN A BOWL OR CONTAINER.
3. PICK ONE.
4. FOLLOW INSTRUCTIONS.
5. REPEAT.

COLOR A PAGE BLACK.	DESCRIBE YOURSELF WITHOUT USING WORDS.	RECORD AN OVERHEARD CONVERSATION.
REMOVE A PAGE.	HIDE THIS IS NOT A BOOK FOR A WEEK.	CREATE AN APPENDAGE FOR THIS IS NOT A BOOK.
COVER A PAGE WITH LINES.	HAVE A FRIEND CHOOSE WHAT PAGE YOU DO NEXT.	WRITE DOWN EVERYTHING IN YOUR HEAD RIGHT NOW.
MAKE A JIGSAW PUZZLE OUT OF PAPER.	TRANSFORM SOME GARBAGE.	LIST ALL OF THE SOUNDS YOU HEAR.

THIS IS AN

IMPERMANENT
OBJECT.

FIND A WAY TO DISPOSE OF
THIS PAGE.

THIS IS A REPETITIVE MOTION.

MAKE THE SAME REPETITIVE MARKINGS TO THE ENTIRE PAGE (E.G., TINY SQUARES, DASHES).

THIS IS A SOUVENIR (OF YOUR TIME SPENT ON THE PLANET). MAKE A LIST OF THINGS YOU MOST ENJOY ABOUT BEING HERE.

THIS A SENSORY DEPRIVATION EXPERIMENT.

1. CLOSE YOUR EYES (OR USE A BLINDFOLD).
2. WALK AROUND YOUR HOUSE OR YARD.
3. DESCRIBE THE EXPERIENCE HERE.

THIS IS A WALL (OR PRIVATE SPACE)

1. OPEN <u>THIS IS NOT A BOOK</u>, STAND IT UP LIKE THIS. →

2. USE IN PUBLIC WHEN A LITTLE PRIVACY IS NEEDED.

3. YOU MAY CUT A HOLE HERE TO SPY IN SOME WAY. →

THIS IS A WALL.

THIS IS A LANGUAGE.

DOCUMENT A JOURNEY USING THE CODES BELOW.
ADD YOUR OWN CODES. TELL A STORY.

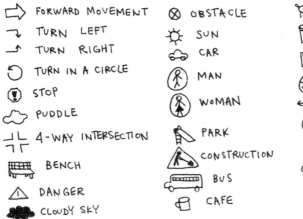

FORWARD MOVEMENT

TURN LEFT

TURN RIGHT

TURN IN A CIRCLE

STOP

PUDDLE

4-WAY INTERSECTION

BENCH

DANGER

CLOUDY SKY

OBSTACLE

SUN

CAR

MAN

WOMAN

PARK

CONSTRUCTION

BUS

CAFE

NICE DOG

GARBAGE

GUERILLA ART

DRINKING FOUNTAIN

BACKTRACK

MEETING PLACE

PLACE TO EXPLORE

TREES

THIS IS A COLLABORATION

1. ASSIGN SOMEONE A GUEST PASS FOR THIS PAGE.
2. INSTRUCT THEM TO ALTER IT IN ANY WAY THEY WISH.

GUEST

NAME:_____

VISITING:_____

DATE:_____   TIME IN:_____   TIME OUT:_____

THIS IS A REPRODUCTION.

1. FILL IN THIS SQUARE WITH PENCIL OR CHARCOAL.
2. CUT ALONG DOTTED LINE. FOLD PAGE LIKE THIS.
3. DRAW SOMETHING. LIFT TO SEE COPY.

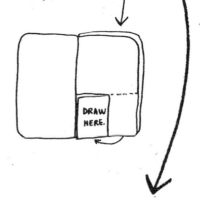

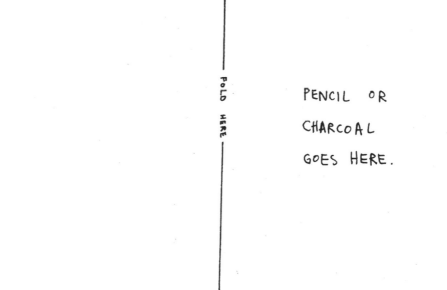

FOLD HERE

PENCIL OR CHARCOAL GOES HERE.

THIS IS A LIST OF OTHER THINGS
THIS IS NOT A BOOK COULD BE.
COME UP WITH YOUR OWN VERSIONS
OF WHAT THEY MIGHT LOOK LIKE.

A PUPPET
A PROTEST
A REVOLUTION
A FORM OF TECHNOLOGY
AN ANSWER TO A QUESTION
A DEBATE
A MICROCOSM
A QUIZ
A SCIENCE EXPERIMENT
A COMMAND
A DIVERSION
A RED HERRING
AN ARTIFICE
A SHIFT IN PERCEPTION
AN IDEOLOGY
A MONUMENT
A MEME
A NEIGHBORHOOD

A TIMELINE
A SPECTACLE
A GIFT
A PRACTICAL JOKE
A MECHANISM
A TIME CAPSULE
A DATABASE
A RUMOR
AN INTERACTION
A CONFESSION
A SEAT
AN ARTICLE OF CLOTHING
THE CENTER OF THE UNIVERSE
AN EXTRAORDINARY EVENT
A DEMONSTRATION OF GRAVITY
A FAKE
AN OUTLINE

NOTES:

RANDOM OCCURRENCE IS AN HOMAGE TO
MARCEL DUCHAMP.

WINDOW IS AN HOMAGE TO YOKO ONO.

CHANCE OPERATION IS AN HOMAGE TO JOHN CAGE.

CONUNDRUM AND TOP SECRET DOCUMENT ARE AN
HOMAGE TO THE OULIPO GROUP.

BUREAUCRACY IS AN HOMAGE TO JOSÉ SARAMAGO.

VOYAGE IS AN HOMAGE TO BAS JAN ADER.

KERI SMITH IS THE AUTHOR
OF SEVERAL BOOKS INCLUDING
WRECK THIS JOURNAL AND
HOW TO BE AN EXPLORER OF
THE WORLD: PORTABLE ART/
LIFE MUSEUM.
READ MORE AT
WWW.KERISMITH.COM.